Ned The Nerdy Narwhal and Friend's

First Day of School!

Written By: Britt Cole   Illustrated by: Kelli Cole

This book is in memory of Jan Kessler.

Thank you for sharing your love of kids and books to the world. Thank you for inspiring me and treating me and everyone you met with such kindness.

For all my kids at St. Boniface Summer Care. Thanks for the amazing summer and fun times! I love and miss you all!

To Radley for being my summer buddy and being the cutest little nerdy toddler I have ever met.

I love you, munchkin!

Today is Ned the Narwhal's first day of school. Mom wakes him up with the news he can wear whatever he wants.

Ned wanted to look cool for all the new friends he would make. So of course, he went through his dress up trunk.

Ned found his favorite superhero cape and mask.

"Are you sure you want to wear that? How about you wear a nice plain shirt?" "No, mama, I am Nerdy Ned the Superhero!"
"Don't call yourself a nerd, honey."
"Why not nerds are cool? We get to be into fun stuff like games and movies and books!"

When he got to his class, the first student he saw was a bull shark. Ned introduced himself "I am Ned, do you want to be my friend?"

"Why would I be friends with you?" The bull shark asked. "You look like a dork... no wait, a nerd!" "Nerds are cool though." Ned said. "Look at my cape; it has my initials on it!"

"Hey Susan, come look at this nerd." Bruce the bull shark shouted. Ned was confused; being a nerd meant knowing a lot, it meant being fun and cool.

"Okay class, everyone get in a circle to Introduce ourselves." Mrs. Dolphin told the class.

"Who wants to go first?" Susan raised her arm. "What did you bring today?" "It's my portable checker set, my mommy made it for me." "That's silly." Bruce not so quietly said, making a few others giggle.

"I think it is cool." Ned said. That made Susan smile. Jane the jellyfish asked to go next. "Look at the face paint my daddy did for me!" "Why did you paint your face, it looks dumb." Bruce snarled. Jane frowned as Mrs. Dolphin told Bruce that he was not being nice.

"I want to go next! "I'm Timothy! I am a hawksbill turtle. Some people think I'm a fatback turtle but my mommy and daddy are both hawksbill turtles so that makes me a hawksbill turtle because they are bot-"
"Do you ever shut up?" Yelled Bruce.
"Bruce, go to time out right now!" Mrs. Dolphin exclaimed.

The day went on with Ned trying not to be bothered by the whispered comments Bruce made when the teachers were not looking. However, at recces, there were so many students and only two teachers that Bruce did not have to be so quiet anymore. "Hey Nerdy Ned the loser! Have you saved the day yet?" The other students gathered around to listen to Bruce talk mean to Ned.

"Nerds are dumb; being a Nerd is for losers."
"No it's not, it's cool and fun and you get to
really be into things you love." Ned explained.
"No, only kelp for brains and weirdos wears
capes!"

"Imma tell Mrs. Dolphin you said that!"
Timothy said from the crowd.

"Don't you dare, shrimp!" Bruce growled.
"I'm a hawksbill turtle, not a shrimp!" Timothy shouted back.
Bruce went to push Timothy.
"You leave him alone!" Ned shouted.

"What are you going to do about it, Nerd?" Bruce rolled his eyes. Knowing that Ned didn't have any real power so he could keep teasing him until he went away.

Ned gathered his inner strength and said. "You are just a bully, I am a superhero and I know how to deal with you." Bruce rolled his eyes again. "What can you do nerd?" Ned struck his best superhero pose. "I am going to be nice, I am going to make friends and we are going to have fun why you be a bully by yourself."

Bruce watched the other kids play together at recess. Everyone looked to be having so much dun. Bruce was starting to realize maybe being different, or loving something so much that you dress up, might not be so bad. Maybe tomorrow he would wear his favorite space hat.

When Ned's mom picked him up from school Ned was so excited he immediately started talking. "Mom it was a great day, I saved the day, and I made lots of friends. One of my friends loves checkers and another one talks a lot but is so funny." Ned was so busy telling all about his day he missed Bruce smiling as he heard the excitement from Ned.

The next day at school. Bruce apologized to all the students he was mean to and showed off his new hat. He also asked Ned to be his friend. From that day on Bruce and Ned were the best and nerdiest of friends.

THE END

Always remember that being different is what makes you special!

Thanks so much for reading and remembering to stay nerdy! For updates on new releases, remember to sign up for my newsletter at TalkBookyToMe.com!

Made in the USA
Middletown, DE
04 July 2018